MW00615248

"Love Cohoes is a working class, to the geographical lines that separate race—and in this verse Gordon bravely tackles the complexities of privilege through her own equally complex identity. 'Cohoes' itself transcends city and becomes a repeated call—no longer a physical place of residence, but beautiful music entering the air as hallelujah."

JD Scott, author of *Funerals & Thrones* (Birds of Lace Press 2013).

"Heroic, elegiac, with a novel-like scope and depth and richness. These poems are warriors carrying full and wounded hearts."

Therese L. Broderick, 2013 overall winner, The Poetry Project with Poetry Ireland, and author of *Dislodged* (Benevolent Bird Press, 2013).

"Elizabeth Gordon digs in and looks for the parts of experience that hold weight, brings them out, holds them up to the light, owns them. That is the beauty of her poetry. She says things that matter."

Dominique Christina, holder of four national poetry titles, author of *The Bones, the Breaking, the Balm: a Colored Girl's Hymnal* (Penmanship Books 2014).

"Elizag [Elizabeth Gordon] gives middle-aged white ladies a bad name. She can wreck it with the best of them."

Taylor Mali, NYC–Urbana, author of *What Teachers Make: In Praise of the Greatest Job in the World* (Putnam 2012).

Love Cohoes

Elizabeth K. Ford

Published by:
Crandall, Dostie & Douglass Books, Inc.
245 West 4th Avenue, Roselle, NJ 07203-1135
(908) 241-5439
www.cddbooks.com

ISBN: 978-1-934390-02-3

To contact the author, send an email to: walk33@gmail.com

For my neighbors

Table of Contents

Part 2—What Grace is For

Acknowledgements

Many of these poems passed through the hands of my Uncommon Grounds writing group. Thank you Julie Gutmann, Jill Hanifan, Sarah Giragosian, and Therese Broderick for so often making it "a good day for poetry." And special thanks to Therese Broderick, the stand-up poet, for reading the manuscript and giving generously of your experience and insight. And thank you Julie for first inviting me to join the group.

This book wouldn't have been written without the ground-breaking, brave existence of Crandall, Dostie and Douglass Books. Thank you Charley Flint and Jeff Hitchcock for believing in me enough to venture into the new territory of poetry.

Thank you Audrey Bennett of Baohouse LLC for the innovative and elegant design.

With gratitude to the following magazines, where these poems first appeared: "If gay marriage had been legal for me" in *Moonshot Magazine*. "The Smell of Gas" also appeared there and was nominated for a Pushcart Prize. "The Clotheslines of Cohoes" in *What Cans't Thou Say*. "Sketch for a Hummingbird" and "Magical Thinking" in *IthacaLit*.

i

ii

Foreword

I moved to Cohoes, a mill city in upstate New York, for the affordable apartments and easy commute to my job across the river in Troy. I discovered a working class white neighborhood not too unlike the ones I had grown up in. And had left. I wanted to leave Cohoes too at first. I sensed and then learned about its reputation as a racist, segregated place—a *bad* neighborhood for my friends and family of color. Could I invite them over? Would they feel safe? Would they be unsafe? Would they think I was reverting to my racist roots, content now to accept the white privilege of being rented to without question?

Wanting to leave, I stayed. For in Cohoes I felt how deep my working class roots went and liked the rooted feeling. My drive to live in multiracial community had been a good one, and I had been wise to follow it. The communities and extended families that I became part of enriched my life, ended the "terrible innocence" Cornel West has described as crippling so many white people, and changed me forever. I tell one story from that season of change in *Walk with Us: Triplet Boys, their Teen parents and Two White Women who Tagged Along*, which this publisher brought out in 2007. But having fled my segregated origins for a more diverse world I had left some work undone, some peace unmade. I had drifted to good places but I was drifting nevertheless. "Be careful when a naked person offers you a shirt," the African proverb warns. If I could not love the people I came from, did I love (understand / accept / forgive) myself?

The day I moved in, a Black girl of five or six and her mother, walking by on their way to the library, stopped to chat. The little girl asked me, "Will you live here for the rest of your life?" As I record in "This Yes," I wanted to say yes. For her, for the fine library she was so pleased to tell me about, for Cohoes. To be there as it grew and changed; to be one of the working class white people who stay and help make King's blessed community not a dream but a place.

To those who feel they live in a post–racial society, this impulse may seem an irrelevant anachronism. So what, they may say, if pockets of segregation have dug their heels deep into the twentieth century? We can leave; we can go to cities where the music is dope and the shops mad hip, where European culture isn't at the center anymore. Perhaps they can leave, can help create new places and not simply versions of the old with better restaurants and more inventive forms of segregation. Perhaps. But I see value in staying.

My first summer here, biking on the rail trail, I drove over two big white words spray-painted across the pavement: *Love Cohoes*. God knows it needs it, I thought, peddling on past a bevy of smoking teenagers. That little girl asking if I would stay, that graffiti flicking beneath my wheels, and my neighbors—their faces and stories, their fears and struggles—invited me into a current of healing, transcending love that is as wide and deep and powerful as Cohoes Falls itself, that most sacred place of the Iroquois nation, cataract the close equal in height, width and water flow to Niagara Falls' American Falls. I was thrilled when I moved in to find the falls so close. I hear the roar from my shared back yard. I can love Cohoes when I try to love Cohoes. Trying takes looking and seeing. Poems look, hard.

Part 1

The Clotheslines of Cohoes

Settling in

So many smokers
I smell dad

So many kettles
I whistle mom

So many potholes
I feel spine

So many leaves
I rustle cousins

So many freight trains
I dream tar sands

So many locks
I rise eerie

The Cats of Cohoes

The man who drove down from Alaska
to start his daughter at the polytechnic
stays, takes 2 cats.

Our landlords, the Cerniaks,
have indoor, outdoor
and fostered cats.

Given the low low rents
and the Cerniaks' relentlessness
most tenants acquiesce to 1 cat

at least. A starter cat.
Some apartments
come with cat.

These June nights, a teenaged girl
broadcasts her orgasms
from the shared hedge. A cat

in heat, Bonnie (3 cats) says,
says she fucks for twenties.
Connie (4 cats)

says *All that shit and fizzle she'll be
knocked up soon enough*

don't worry. Two months here I (1 cat)
finally see the white skunk
nosing for grubs by moonlight,
a skunk who likes the cats

of Cohoes, Helen (allergic)
tells me, a skunk who only sprays
drunks and teenaged girls.

This Yes

*When the federal government required the mills of Cohoes to
hire "colored" workers or lose war contracts, the mills relented
but Cohoes maintained its segregation. Workers of color settled
across the river in North Troy.*

I cross the rivers people crossed to get to work: Hudson
then Mohawk coming, Mohawk
then Hudson going.
Scenic.

I can't feel it: river as moat, bridge as fence, labor as white
privilege; can't hate Cohoes the way red-lined lives
must have hated
Cohoes.

The day I move in a Black girl of five or six stops to chat
and chatting asks, "Will you live here
the rest of your life?"
I feel

invited, invoked, inclined toward yes. Oh shaded streets!
Her mother and I touched glances in silent,
cynical assessment:
This

is no place to live a whole life. But didn't dappled shade,
enthusiastic child, even silent, cynical
agreement disagree?
Yes.

Scenic Cohoes, I felt this yes.

Drops the Spine

One man, one heron, fishing from the rocks
where the third branch of the Mohawk
rounds Peebles Island and
drops

into a whetstone stretch. The man leaves first.
The heron stands still so long I hunger
for a hunger that quells
the spine

of every feather. Sewage spirals in an eddy,
brown, ocher, cochleal...
The heron resolves
into dusk

and sometime later lifts and glides to the shal-
lows, slight, elusive sail
above the solid
hull

of its shadow. The Milky Way's our longest
throat. If I can't be still I'll be
the fish stillness
caught.

Drops the spine into dusk's hull, caught.

For a Place

Yes, I live on The Hill. Yes
in the old mill houses.

The professor emeritus
born across from closed St. Agnes's
in the house with the last elm tree, can't believe
someone who teaches where he taught
lives where he lived
five decades and three degrees ago.

I'm an adjunct, contingent labor,
and why I live here professor is complicated and
very simple: I make $3,000 a course
at three courses max per term
and my rent on a decent one-bedroom
is $425 a month plus
cold makes everything worse.

Basic math, like a sum
growing in your head as groceries fill the basket.
Then again men of your generation generally
didn't
shop for groceries
did they?

But you had a mother

and that mother had a depression
and that depression had a father kneeling
to light the votive candle of a sapling
whose eventual vaulted arches
survived, shaded my Hyundai

the day I came shopping
for a place
to save what I've saved.

Love Cohoes

Powerball Quickdraw Quick 5 Take 10
Megamillions Sweet Millions State
Minimums on ALL
Cigarettes

Price Chopper shoppers slung with slender
tanks of oxygen. On the rail trail teens
smoking and making
memories

We hear without hearing
      mice scream
as their hearts are pierced
      by our cats

See without fearing
      our neighbors'
dream cleaver TV's deep
      into the night

Fear without fleeing
      mid-week
workers drunk and
      stoned again

Wake without waking
        craving only
what money (what
        genius!) can buy

All the heavy
machinery of Cohoes
driven by white men

I just noticed

Baby strollers
driven by the Black men
white women chose

Sewer
the sign says   Project

        state money
for the Harmony Mills
        Luxury Apartments
We know we won't get better service

We only hope they leave us some

❖ ❖ ❖

Love Cohoes
blips beneath my bike tire

message
like a crosswalk
I'm crossing
wrong way first, x axis
     over
            y

Co–
   as in
      coauthor
         coagulate
             codependent
                   coexistence
                        co (I'm
            trying

                          to

                    love you)

                                           hoes

America the Beautiful, America the Tomb

Caught in the canyon of rowhouses,
held in the nets of our remnant orchard
comes a roar like rush hour traffic more
rushed after rain, somehow organic.

A power's here, strumming the clotheslines,
calling me down the hill mill workers walked
to get to work. Oh happy accident:
to have found an apartment with white noise

of actual white water of waterfall rivaled
this half of the continent only by Niagara.
One gaze can't take in both banks, nor words
convey the void beauty of the bars of shadow

flood plain tree trunks cast upon the mist
that rises from Pleistocenic gorge,
rises and gazes back at the waters
that made it, like a child contemplating

a parent's face, like America facing
its violence. One gaze can't take in both
past and present, nor words demolish
the gallows of responsibility and guilt

from which I take in the view. Oh sacred
test: to hear within the roar of Cohoes Falls
the robot buzz of American drones, to love
beauty yet hold truth close as a throbbing

tooth. Eighty thousand Americans in steel
cages no sound but crashing steel reaches,
Herman Wallace forty–two years
in the hole, SHU, and innocent, and dying

today (home of the brave) after three
days free. Dying today after three days free.

Patriotic

Fireworks start here on Memorial Day
and all the parks are memorial parks.

Feeling so American, so free, so able
to give up power in order to live

in a world where the children have eaten.

Know Thyself

The Obama sticker on my bumper comes with conver-
sation requirement. Most days I'm
willing. Some days
I remember

rifle barrels bristling from station wagons (afterschool
pickup) or the anti-bussing rally my
mother's new friend
dragged

us to. We'd just moved in, hadn't learned yet whom to
hate. I thought the bleachers might
collapse. I thought the
Black boys

my father drove to and from football so we'd win but
keep our side of State Road 7 white were
cuter, nice.
Feeling

safe here isn't. My first Black teacher, a Mr. Spinks,
told me Know thyself. Like Oedipus I had to
know my parents first.
Jesus

told me Love thy neighbor. Could be it's an a b thing: a)
Know my own racism, my roots, my culpable,
cowardly silences; b) Love
my neighbor.

I remember dragged Black boys. Feeling Jesus, my neighbor.

Secondhand Smoke

Kathy lives beneath me, drinks and drinking
smokes so much I'm smoking with her. Air
purifiers contaminate the quiet and anger's
an added carcinogen. Matthew, her brain
injured son, stands out so long in the rain
one day I ask does he need help. The answer
is slow to come: He lost his key, his mother's
at work. Anyway, it's a light rain he waits in.

What engineer can ever navigate the drop
between ageless love and the second hand of rage?
Will the God who told the glacier where to stop,
who stretched an arm of water and tore the gorge
from bedrock let me in anyway? Does thought
redeem anything? Can doors be opened with a page?

What I Hate About Cats

1

How on entering
they must sniff the doorsill
every time
as if cougars
supped here
as if dogs drop by for tea

2

How they never
wash the cat food bowl
ever, or even leave it to soak

3

How they retch and puke
then go back to sleep
beside the squib of puke

4

How though they are purported to be intelligent
they never warn you about the squib of puke

5

How their bodies sliding along your leg
remind you you have never swum with dolphins
and don't want to
and what kind of a person is it
who doesn't want to swim with dolphins?

Breathing

Waterfalls round the clock spittin' out negative ions dude like
WWE wrestlers talkin' shit and those ions I'm tellin' you
body slam all type particlelate matter, purifying the crap out the air.

Plus also stimuslating (google it) sero-yeahbaby-tonin production.
Bitch let me see you be depressed now!

No wonder kids still go down to the river to smoke.
No wonder the hill's thick with SSI.
No wonder the back porches of Cataract Street
lean toward the falls.

My old man drove truck with a Mohawk guy who told him
he used to swim there, yeah before the power plant, before the razor wire, before
I forget which war. How close to the cascadance he didn't say but
claimed, claimed as a subsequence special powers

of flight. Could see through an eagle's eyes what an eagle sees. See dude the eagle is mad sacred to the Indian way of feeling. He cracked my dad a good one down to Joe's and that was that.

All I'm saying is dude, dude! could be we're being jizzled 24/7 by some kinda helladope hydro-healing secret ion mechanichism! Not vacuum up your damn data type secret but deer sipping from a stream type secret, eagle on the powerline and you think dang, big hawk type secret.

I mean we may be Walking Dead fans breaking bad bread daily but least we're breathing, breathing, me 'n you dude I'm tellin' you we're breathing some seriously decrassified O^2 blue.

G Major

Beech, maple, pear, apple, hemlock
in a shared backyard.

Recycling buckets like big blue Legos
someone didn't pick up.

A picnic table with decomposing legs
listing prow-ward, years from sinking.

In the fence along the alley
four gates rusted open.

In summer housecats at most
every screen, lean strays spraying the shrubs.

The stained glass windows of St. Agnes's
strapped to the sides of a white van.

A girl with Down Syndrome calling
"Hey I got a guitar! I play a G major!"

The minor chord months, November
through March, December

a bush of burning nights.

The Clotheslines of Cohoes
After Allen Ginsberg's "America"

Cohoes, the ropes of your clotheslines are rotting!
Don't you want to smell the Great Lakes in your sheets anymore Cohoes?
Don't you want the sun to puff the turned-out pockets of your Dockers?
Dear Cohoes, we're in trouble. Be honest: how many days before you open your utility bill?
Kim Jong Un wants your clotheslines Cohoes. Him wants them stiff iron posts, them balls of cement.

America's got talent, talent and clothespins.

Lucille told me Cohoes how you used to tell stories as you hung out your clothes,
kids running through the arms of a whole building's shirts, empty lines on wash day signaling trouble
    bad trouble in the house.

I think tenements were little villages.
I think you're a little ashamed Cohoes. I don't get it, you're so pretty.

Is it because they look like crosses two stories high? Is it because people say Cohoes is poor?

Oh Cohoes don't listen to gossip! They do look like crosses two stories high and we are poor!

That man who owns the laundromat? He's not happy.

Don't worry Cohoes, I'll take in your clothes if it storms when you at Walmarts.
I won't count holes in your socks or notice what brand undies you buy.
I don't guess you buy the same brand Anthony Weiner buys but how can I ever know for sure Cohoes
   if you let your clotheslines rot?

One clothespin holds two shoulders, remember? Jeans dry last. Pulleys squeaking as a load's run out early
morning and back in afternoon or evening mark time much better than daytime TV.
Did you think of the bedridden and debilitatingly depressed when you let your clotheslines rot Cohoes?

I'll tell you a secret: all Lucille's sheets are white, white and perfect, sailboats at the starting line,
   ironed clouds, clan robes in detox.

Oh Cohoes, I want to look up from doing dishes to see the prayer flags of your tank tops.
I want to feel guilty for sleeping when you've done two loads already.
I want to compete with you Cohoes.
I want to hang my clothes better and faster.

I want them to snap all dust bowl in the wind.
And I want to concede defeat to you Cohoes.
I want to say "You're a better housewife than I am Cohoes."

Show me the prom dress,
the cribsheet,
the tablecloth,
the robe washed for a last time.

Show me your stains and I'll show you mine.

Meanwhile sunlight wicks the dew from every blade.
Meanwhile breezes dry the hair of the drowned and fill the shirt sails of the most desperate sailors.

I have a shawl I want to show you Cohoes.

Look at me when I'm loving you Cohoes!
My mother speaks to me from the grave.
She tells me you sell those dryers downriver,
sell those damn dryers to Yonkers.

Come outside Cohoes. Come on out.
Tell those chump squirrels—these ain't no tightropes!
Tell National Grid—get your greed out my pocket.
    Tell your children—two shoulders one clothespin, thus.

On Mangam Street

There's a beautiful pothole on Mangam Street.
You could reach most of a forearm in and touch
the cobblestones of a century two centuries

past. Unmortared stones, laid in sand, give
and settle when frost heaves the ground, superior
to pavement and a vast improvement over

the mud and ruts of dirt roads. Plus cobblestones
warn walkers of iron wheels approaching.
We know the clop–clop from old movies

but can we see a young man standing in a stream,
pants wet to the knees, big hands in among
the rounded stones choosing?

A tumbrel on the bank takes the weight
of lobbed stones and the stones score their first song,
sound track to a fantasy jaunt he takes as he works—

through the orchard we still call orchard
though it's Vleit Street now and the apples few,
then on to lace the alleyways of the hill like a lady's boot,

his flatbed wagon (for fire wood, vegetables later),
his strong horse, shod hooves clapping like the applause

of the woman who'll choose him not for his muscles
though his muscles are lovely but for the pennies
his labor lays down, a road straight to the grandchildren
and great—my neighbors on Mangam Street.

#writtenatcohoesfalls
after lines by Thomas Moore

From rise of morn until sunset I have heard the mighty Mohawk run,
like a washing machine at a summer camp, like a child's heart
transplanted into a marathoner.

Practice Cohoes Lacks

The barrel maker who went over Niagara in a barrel
to prove the strength of his barrel's staves
went over Cohoes Falls first.
Practice.

And we had tourists once too, a cable car, a Cataract
Inn whose windows opened on magnificence.
Is it self esteem or imagination modern
Cohoes lacks?

At least the latest company to lease the Mohawk's
flow was asked to grant access. Access
is a bridge across the power canal,
a walkway

down to the base of the falls. That walkway's steep
and often closed. You could drown in the surge
from a storm far away
the way

the history of a place floods the present of that place
and flattens people like grasses that are flattened
but not necessarily
drowned.

Practice Cohoes lacks, a walkway the way drowned.

The Great Peacemaker

When we know a people by the name their enemies gave them
what do we know? The Narragansett called them Mohawk,
Man Eaters. They called
themselves

Kanien'keha, *People of the light or of the flint*, and their home
Ga-ha-hoose, *White Pine* (to Dutch ears *Cohoes*).
And if we should hear
the sacred

story of a people ours endeavored to destroy what do we hear?
He canoed alone from Lake Skanyadario, *Beautiful
sheet of water*, built a greeting
fire

and waited. Runners came, the people heard his message: Bury
your weapons of war, let women choose the leaders,
listen to the voice
within.

They put him in the tallest white pine, high above the falls. Flint
found its heart and tree and man fell to the froth below.
A trial to prove his prophesy
true

or not. I have stood on that cliff, have asked the ground for a trace
of that tree, have wondered what branches of faith
he clutched as he fell.
Dawn's

sun rose on a stem of smoke. Runners came. If Mary Magdalene,
at the mouth of the tomb, looked she might have seen
a guardian eagle,
skajina.

Themselves the sacred beautiful. Within true dawn, skajina.

What My Uncle Billy Remembered

Leaflets clutched to his chest like a sweater
the son of a Vilna Talmudist braves the Irish
tenements. Billy's mother lets him in. A crucifix
skims from piecework's bulb. What many remember
is rats. Hands are crushing the masses! Again her
mind gulls off to the cairn in far Limerick,
glass ever raised for hers: To Themselves, Patrick
and Gaven, the older then the younger brother

crushed in the trenches that promised bread
and a manliness stolen fields alone could cede.
The lesser Diaspora, Ireland's. Still, stone
for the souls come home and their last lastdime
fierce to the bone of a stranger's palm—Take it,
mother of God use it—what Billy remembers of hope.

The Spinner's Prayer

Is it a fool they take me for?
You couldn't cook a rat in that damn thing.
Why 'tis all I can do to get a kettle boiling for tea
in the morning if ever they left me
time in the morning for tea.

Now the hearth back home—
you could roast a hindquarters entire in it
with room for a kettle big as a milking pail
and a pot of stew fit to feed a family of ten
come in from the haying.

Big as a tomb it was in the end. Grief
for stew, tears the tea. I'll not ask your pity.
We came for food, we found food enough.
The rest we figured to be a pack of lies
and it was.

At the looms we stand one wall to the other
like tines in a rake to rake a county clean
of tenants. Across the river the puddlers and molders
talk strike. I believe they will strike, for last August
the heat took three and here it is, July.

My father was the one found my brother,
did I tell ye? him and his darling Mary

frozen in a ditch, grass juice greening
their mouths, her with her hands in the rags
of his chest, like his heart was the last coal of winter.

I'm from Mayo God–help–us
and in Mayo God–help–us
it's road building they put the paupers to
and those roads go nowhere.
If I go back, and I'll not go back,

I'll stand on the roadway my parents built
and I'll follow it by God to the poorhouse
that gave them food enough to lift a shovel
but food too little to live. I'll burn it down
if I go back and I'll not go back

but it warms me now as I work at the loom
to think of the flames covering the lice
and the stinking buckets, feeding sparks
to the starved moon. 'Tis a small joy
to picture my brother and his darling Mary

rising from their bed in the frozen bog,
like bride and groom walking
to the altar of the fire.
Oh it seems to me now the heart

of the Blessed Virgin herself I'm seeing.

Is it she who'll return our families to us?
I pray for my bitterness to have an end,
that I see no more in the mill manager's eyes
the eyes of the landlord who put us out
in the winter of death,

that I hear no more in the overseer's voice
the voice of the man who let me and my sisters,
our mother and father into the poorhouse
but turned away my brother and his darling Mary.
His heart's last heat not enough. Yet given,

given. Oh there's days I would hold
all the world's freezing to my breast,
and days I would set the mill on fire,
days I would set the mill
on fire.

Depression—1873–1877

We told them
cut the hours not the pay
if there's too much cloth on the market.

They cut the pay but not the rents
and they weathered the storm
like the storm itself.

In 1880 we struck
and their model factory, their happy family,
two-thirds of us girls
under twenty, spoke as one:

Cut the hours not the pay
if there's too much cloth on the market.

The Spinner's Retort

Mr. Robert Johnston sir, you call us family.
It may well be that the saloons and churches,
schools and stores, city hall itself (for now)
and all our houses are owned by the mill.
It well may be that I am but a drop of water
in the canal that turns your Rolsten Turbines

but I'll have you know sir your grand turbines
will not be swallowing my God given family.
I never thought I'd be grateful for the wide water
between them and me but I am. As for your churches
Mr. Johnston, they're as Protestant as your mill.
I never was a souper sir and I won't become one now.

In the west of Ireland is a cairn I see clearly now.
It stands on a crumbling cliff where the turbines
of greed have long powered the looms of a mill
whose product is grief. There you'll find my family.
A blighted crop and export ships, churches
silent as starved counties. Cross the waters

of the Great Hunger, cross the dreadful waters
of Lethe sir if you would be kin to me. Stop now
with your talk. We sing in separate churches.
Your wealth grows with each day your turbines
turn, while the girls and women of my family
are worn to a welt of weary by every mill

day. Don't think me ungrateful for work at the mill.
Back home a brook a quarter–mile off gave us water,
a cow milk and butter, the soil too poor for a family
of ten. And my mother with no No to speak of. Now
I can see beyond this season of looms and turbines;
can see, as on a clear day, the spires of far churches,

better lives for my children. For me, it's the church's
graveyard. I know wherefrom I come. Not this mill.
I am more than the froth spit from your turbines.
I am the river from which you siphoned the water.
It flows to profit none and to serve all. What now
Mr. Robert Johnston? Would you call me family

still? Then let us enter the churches of the water.
My anger once longed to set your mill on fire; now
love gentles its turbines. I see all, all are family.

The Spinner's Defense

My grandniece here, my sister's son's only girl,
is after telling me the streets of Cohoes
were paved with the sweat and blood of the Blacks.

Well they weren't paved with gold, I'll grant her that.
But we walked them happy enough on our day off.
You'd've walked on pig shit after the six twelve–hour days.

Herself here thinks reading and writing's work.
I'll grant it's work if there's a paycheck in it
but if you've spit enough at the end of the day to complain
of the wrongs of a day long gone
then I've this to say to ya: work harder.

It came to me some days...the old hearth, folks close
against the cold, stories, songs, always someone
quick with the fiddle or the penny whistle.

It came to me...the smell of the sea,
the keening sound of the wind.

The roar of the looms washed most of Mayo God–help–us away
and what's left of it I'll not speak of here.

If I've the blood and sweat of the Blacks on my boot soles
as her ladyship claims why I'll number it among my many regrets
but I'll add this: I fed the ones it was left to me to feed.
I took the work there was for me to take.

I did nay know them in the south were taken by the work,
no strike but escape, no quitting but dying,
their very darling babies a figure in the manager's book.

I had not eyes to see the blood on the cotton I spun.

My cousin Dehlia Laegan did I tell ye went home to Mayo
and lives there still? Sure the coffin ships had room enough
going back.

The slave ships I expect would have filled.
Or it could be some would have liked my job at the mill,
my wage, my Sunday stroll along Mohawk Street,
not paved with gold but God help me
smooth enough.

The Sea Knew a Small Sigh

The ships that brought us, they were slavers first. Coffin ships
we called them for it's that they were for many a one,
shackles scraping like fingers
at a coffin

lid, sliding and scraping in the lurch and roll of the sea. 'Twas
how in the below decks night you knew you lived.
And the ghosts of the Africans
groaning,

groaning and praying and bodies raining, escaping into the sea.
I hear it I tell you, I hear it still. Whisht now girl
and you may hear it too.
The sea,

in a placid mood, sighs like a lover when the finger of a body
enters. My cousin Dehlia, too sick herself with fever
to raise her head heard,
knew

her baby gone. Delirium, a fine word, but educated as you are
you'll not learn the Latin root of how a mother
comes to hear such
a small sigh.

At the looms we heard only the looms, a skeleton's reel. Nights
we heard those falls. The name comes they say
from a Mohawk family
falling

over the edge. Over the edge of famine my people poured, more
than the waters that turn the turbines, less than the sea
that opens for babies and Africans
free.

At a coffin groaning the sea knew a small sigh, falling free.

One Light for Lucille

To reach my basement storage, my bin of Christmas, I've got to go through
Lucille's kitchen at the far end of this four-unit building.
She's a widow, past seventy, five-foot
(just),

keeps solar powered figurines (dollar store plastic) bobbling in her window.
She was born and raised in Cohoes, both parents at the mill,
on different shifts, but
don't

pity her; she had her Me-Meh in the house, Arcadian French was spoken,
the food was very good. My first time down she went along
backward-crawling on the steep,
narrow

steps. Hands to my shoulders she guided me through the grotto of conjoined
cellars to each hidden light: one a modern switchplate, one
a sort of doorbell with a brown, furzy cord,
one

a porcelain ring 'round a ball-shaped bulb. Through eras of lighting fixtures
we went until a slatted wooden bench cobweb grey and half
hidden under cardboard set Lucille's face a-
light.

My Me-meh's, I can't bear to throw it away. I saw kindling, nothing more,
looked again, saw glossy teak at the center of a garden,
a solid old woman patting it, calling
for Lucille,

Lu, to come, come and sit. Saw Christmas times and the bench a low altar
offering packages from the skirt of a lit tree, Lucille in PJ's
descending, sparking three generations'
joy.

Just don't narrow one light. For Lucille, joy.

Cross

Is understanding why you can't love someone a bridge to loving or the beginning of despair? (Always more bad news about my character, my failings, my waywardness, my "refusals, hates, postponements, meanness, laziness," to lift from Whitman's "Crossing Brooklyn Ferry"). I don't know. I think most addiction, and the less deadly dissipation, is recoil from this understanding plus a wise assessment of what love would have meant, could have *done*.

We filled our sled with Christmas packages and drove it off a cliff. Broken in the wreckage we open what we can reach. Understanding why you can't love someone is a bridge to loving. Cross it, don't look down. Cross it.

Today doing dishes I thought of the movie *Children of Men*, of the scene where the only woman to give birth in twenty-odd years walks with her infant through an urban battle. The refugees under attack—refugees—by the British army hear the crying baby, and we hear sighs and prayers in many languages. Mother and child and one brave escort come down the soon to be destroyed stairs into the soldiers. They too are quieted, stunned, a few crying, a few praying. The baby changes everything, for a moment. And then nothing: the battle resumes.

Doing the dishes I was crying thinking how every baby born is a Christ child Buddha entering this war zone, every baby's cry a call to cease fire and live in peace. "Trailing clouds of glory do we come, from God, who is our home." Daily, hourly, the sacrilege and tragedy. All over the world. When I watched the movie, that scene struck me as implausible—that the soldiers did not lay down their weapons and weep with gratitude and joy for the apparent salvation of the human race. Don't you think they would have? I mean had there been no infant born anywhere on earth in twenty years?

And we should, for there's been no infant innocence and hope at the heart of many hearts for some time; not since the last war, the last rape, the last lie, the last theft by government or corporation or by the two working in tandem.

Do I hear the newborn infant crying in Cohoes? Do I lay down my gun, my judgment, my clever assessments and analysis? Do I cover the mother in prayers and sighs, leaving my fears and desires, ambitions and aversions, in order to walk in the light of a purpose?

A humble purpose, as befits this hill, this shut down company town, this sacred white pine place above the falls, this column of smoke rising saying Come, I have words to speak and from those words might come, if you listen, peace.

Understanding why you can't love someone is a bridge to loving. Some bridges feel like a sudden and steep drop into thunderous water. Cross anyway. Fall anyway.

A Heron I Know

On most any walk or drive
the Hudson's sunny muscles

one branch then another of the Mohawk

ducks snicking the current
geese like stones
and when water everywhere else
is frozen eagles
feeding below the falls

today a heron
a heron I know

Part 2

What Grace is For

First date

After Andrea Gibson's "Too Much"

I want to know if you peeked when you played hide and seek
I want to know what you see when you look within
I want to unbutton your house and reach in
I want to know how many inches
your laugh is and how fast you can change
a life

Or do you hate corny questions like that
like *What is your biggest accomplishment?*
I want to know your biggest color
your favorite fear
your happiest donut
and if you ever drank too much
perfume.

I want to know what you'd say if I told you
that as I write this I spy a squirrel
sitting atop a telephone pole *eating it*, I mean
going ham on that treated lumber. Would you
a) doubt it
b) wonder if I have ADD
c) make a joke, as in 'how many squirrels *does* it take
        to eat a telephone pole?'

d) ask if I got off my lazy poet-ass and gave that poor squirrel
        something to eat? or
e) c and d above (ooh, funny *and* kind...maybe it is love)

If it *is* love I'm gonna need to know
if you ever tried to fly
if you ever launched your body
from a bunkbed a gargoyle a Wednesday.
Did you ever play spin the bottle with the full moon
and a steel drum spitting fire? And who broke your start?

Or do you hate personal questions like that
like: *How old were you when you first had sex?*
I want to know how bold you were
when you first met death: Did you kiss it
did you floor it did you linger in the hallway?

Too intense? Just tell me then what you sing on road trips
and what's the longest hope you ever took
and how far you're willing to go
for a cat

Or do you hate hypothetical questions like that
like *Where will you be in ten years?*
I want to know where you'll be in ten miracles
I want to know if you ever carved your name in bubbles

I want to meet your toes some time in a bright alley
I want to know the distance between the tip of your middle finger
and the tip of my iceberg
I want to know the first question
your last lover asked you
and the last words you said
to the first pet who died on you

Or do you hate sad questions like that?
I *like* it that you hate sad questions like that
I think I wanna swallow your sun
I wanna have your daisy
I wanna hang pictures on your tomorrow
I wanna unclench your past tense   real
slow down now   it's only

                    a first date

A Rack of Bagels

At the table of the established
poetry group, coffee, cappuccino, chai, me invited, impressed.

A skinny woman not twenty
hurries past, a rack the size of my writing table
hefted on her shoulder.

Fresh bagels.
This place is known for its bagels.

We thresh poems
about the care of linen
a fish that lives
within man–o–war tentacles
childhood trauma as
Christmas package and
an army ant addressing the housecats.

She glides through again,
six-foot of aluminum ladder
balanced well on her hip.

The one arm
hooked 'round a rung   the auburn braid
lyrical along her hairline

surpass
our efforts   remind me
I come from servants
servant girls

Mariah MacDonald   Elizabeth Mellett
Katie Gordon and my mother   Catherine Zita
who did twelve rooms a day until one day

she couldn't. O give us this day
our daily ladder
and deliver us from ego.
For thine is the coffee bean
and the tea leaf
thine the everything bagel

poems but racks we carry
with what grace
we can   Word
without end

amen

Whose Clocks

My mother used to
      light cigs off a tipped
             toaster

Did her eyelids
  glow,
      did her pie wedge
    of browscar?—*numb*   she told us
                go ahead

     touch it

How could we know
if touch got through?

She limped on a short crooged leg
Her laughter chunged into coughs
Just last week her sister told me
she answered the phone
Widow with five children here

How could she know
it was her sister calling?

Everyone loved her
She had a violent temper
She let things happen
She did twelve rooms a day
      at the Berkshire Hilton
          until she couldn't

then hospitals and *no tubes*!
then tubes and
home and
that question
Whose clocks are those?

How could she know
she was a collector of clocks?

A girl with long auburn hair
  leans on the red brick of a Bronx stoop
    one saddle shoe heel   on the toe of the other

                    breasts new
              waist narrow
                          smile
          almost mine

The Smell of Gas

In 1979..., while Exxon's net income rose 56 percent to more than 4 billion,
three-thousand small independent gasoline stations went out of business.
—from Howard Zinn's *A People's History of the United States*

At the intersection of A1A and Sunrise Boulevard
my best friend Fred pumped gas at his dad's station,
squeegied windshields smartly, wiper arms popping the glass
like bras on girls' backs,

his uniform pants creased clean as palm frond edges,
the letters of his name stitched in gold above his pocket.
Fred had a car before I had my license,
the Beatles' every album.

A motel maid found his father. The bullet had exited
out the back, like with JFK except Fred's father
lived, did custodial work, eyelid
jammed in a wink, suicide attempt

a speck on a blip in a system built to powerlift
the few, the rest of us crouched in fumes ratcheting handjacks,
Fred loving the smell of gas, inheriting
that

Are You Really Working Class? Test Yourself

Ever shopped at Walmart—1 point

Ever worked at Walmart—3 points...per year

Ever washed more than hands and face in Walmarts bathroom—4 points

Never been in Walmarts—lose 5 points

Followed by store clerks a lot and you're white—1 point

Followed by store clerks a lot and you're black—no points, obviously

Age at first dentist visit: 10 years or older—1 point

15 or older—2 points

25 or older—Yo you have a dental phobia try hypnosis. But
if that visit was for an abscess and your face was swole out like a turned over cereal bowl—bonus point
if your face was swole out like a turned over cereal bowl and your grandmother gave you a swig a
whiskey and told you swish it around and quit your goddamn whining—double bonus
if you swallowed after you swished and liked that bloody whiskey...priceless

Age at first real vacation...Aw quit your damn whining

Did you ever have to sleep in your car—one point

That car didn't lock—2 points

Ever had sex with someone to avoid sleeping in your unlockable car—3 points. But,
if that someone was lovely and a safe harbor and made buckwheat pancakes with real maple syrup
    in the morning maybe that was the point

Childhood dogs all unspayed, unneutered, and untrained—1 point
Childhood dog ran off and you found him and snatched him away from a slathering pack
    to save him from becoming a rapist – 5 points! No I'm giving you 10!
That dog was named Hennessey – holy crap what a coincidence, proof of parallel universes—point, set
    match

Own a coat that cost less than twenty dollars—1 point
It's your only coat—2 points
It's my grandad's coat – holy Macklemore, that is fucking awesome

Ever had a fight in a bar—1 point
Ever banned from a bar for fighting—2 points...per bar
Wanna fight me now over class stereotypes in this poem—no points, and fuck you!

Ever hitch–hiked to get to work, jumped a turnstile to get to work, drove on empty to get to work,
drove while picking your nose to distract oncoming state trooper from expired inspection sticker

to get to work—1 point each (and that last one really works)

Pipes ever froze and burst—3 points...per winter. But
if there was a brook nearby,
if you broke the ice on that brook
with a ker-thunk of your splitting maul
and hauled water bucket by moon-bobbling bucket back,
let me point out you were rich, rich beyond measure

Ever lost a parent better health care might have saved—No point holding onto that bitterness
Weren't there other factors? Don't suffering and death come to all classes?

Ever went barefoot in summer—half a point
went barefoot in winter—wow! Give yourself whatever
went barefoot to school—dang! 10 points
Slammed barefoot. No points!

Feel shame now when someone checks out your shoes—1 point
Feel shame when you have to re-swipe—1 point
Feel shame when you add up your score here and see how <u>high</u> it is—1 point

Feel envy when you add up your score and see how low it is—No points...*aw* quit your damn whining, I'll give you the point, but don't bullshit me because I can look you in the eye and see you never washed your ass in a Walmart sink

Now what you gonna do with your points? If you have over 30, over 40, take a pointer from someone over 50—let 'em go. That's right, let 'em go like a fistful of helium balloons so people everywhere can look up and point at everything you have overcome.

Adult Low Dose

You could read anything.
You could read the back of an aspirin bottle.
                                    —Open mic host

1

Facts: minor delayed action
will keep children and teenagers
alert and bleeding

Pregnant professionals
exceed water, exceed Skokie

  Illinois

Immediate   complete
         drug therapy
       recommended

                              a full glass

              not to exceed each
                      safety-coated
                         adult

❖

Active needing
recommended by your doctor

not this pox
not this syndrome

                              but serious   liver

          serious use

2

Under the Sink is More Optimistic
(if you're green)

Friendlier, upright, free—no
swallowed eyes, no
vomiting machine

❖

Free love   with book cases
clean   natural excess

no reach required
no residue dulling the years

❖

Once empty   you are
          entire

the trusted miracle

Carpenter's Helper

It was below zero eighteen days running
the winter of 1994 in Brattleboro, Vermont,
when to ground myself in my body
and not float away so much
I talked my way into a carpenter's helper job.

The warehouse was supposed to have been
closed in by Thanksgiving but the architects
put the windows in the wrong places
and so we were out on the scaffolding
framing windows, framing windows
in the below zero wind.

They let me carry heavy stuff
because I was the helper not the carpenter
but they showed me how to carry it:
Plywood you grab dead center, one hand on top, one on bottom,
    and if it's windy, *tip it. Tip it. Tip…it!*

Sheetrock the same but don't ding the edges
   on the *watch the studs will ya!*
And lumber—squat and settle a bundle
on your shoulder then stand and *atta boy, er girl*

Drunk or sober Jack could slap together a flight of stairs
by lunch but *best leave Jack be.*

Danny, crew chief, philosopher by nature,
mysterious nerve damage to hands,
face lines burred with crosstie cracks.
Handsome and quiet, fair.

Roth, the little guy, showing palms stained brown
by lacquer: "I won't have to do these hands again for a month."
Short and poor, hurt, dangerous, chewing racism
like a good plug.

And Marcus, philosopher by training (Amherst),
cured existential any dilemma with

Make something every day.
Feared no height
dropped no weight
measured *and* cut once.

I bought a new tool every paycheck:
tool belt, claw hammer, rip hammer, nailset,
tape measure, cats paw, chalkline, tri-square,
straight square, level.

They let me carry heavy stuff
because I was the helper not the carpenter
but they showed me how to carry it,
taught me that a nail gun is a rabid dog
that waiting is working if you're always ready to *move it*
that plywood has to fly off a truck like cards out of a dealer's hands
that paint can be applied at way below the recommended temperature
that a rip hammer stops a slide from a steep-pitched roof
but *better whang that thing in deep!*
that laughter at lunch can save the day

that guys don't share food
that guys don't leave early
that guys don't get sick
that everyone pulls their weight
and everyone weighs more
after 2:00 o'clock

I imagine some of them are dead.
It was so long ago.
My tool belt's stiff.
My hammer's a different one.
It hardly goes below zero
anymore.

Are you alright
you men of my construction season?
A few years when I learned
my body was on the earth and the earth
is steeply pitched so *pay the fuck attention!*
Are you alright

you carpenters who I helped?
Do you remember me?
Did I help you?

The Day and the Hour of His Death

On the day and in the hour when John F. Kennedy
was shot I was in the fourth row of Sister Anthony's
first grade class looking through the tall, many-paned
windows at the convent. I believed the president was in
there, the stamen of a flower with praying sisters as the
petals because Sister Anthony had told us the nuns were
in the convent praying for him and where else would they
bring the first Catholic president when he was shot but
to St. Peter's Catholic School in Monticello, New York? My
world was so small.

On the day and in the hour when Martin Luther King
Junior was shot I was...I don't remember where. No one
I knew wept, none prayed. No childish misunderstanding
barnacles the ship of the story. Even that babbler, our TV,
was all Twilight Zone, wonderful world of color-lessness
coating the days of our children.

In November 1968 we moved to Florida. I-95 was a dot-
ted line in places back then and we got lost in the spaces,
found ourselves on a red road in Georgia, a Black child
before a bare shack open down the center with the sunset
shining gold down the center and a gold-lit tree conspir-
ing with the light to speak, *You will remember that you do
not remember the day and the hour of his death.*

April 4 1968, 6:01 PM. Take My Hand, Precious Lord, his last request. People everywhere crying, crying and praying, and maybe somewhere a young child gazing at a hill she takes to be a mountain, at a cloud she mistakes for a hand. Precious Lord. The day and the hour, the death.

Addition and Subtraction

Two facts that don't add up: 1) Experts estimate 11
Sandy Hook schoolchildren were saved when Adam Lanza
stopped to load a new 20-bullet magazine; 2) Four
months later, 54 senators voted against a law limiting
magazines to 10 bullets.

Two rooms
full of soft, warm bodies
asking questions, learning
addition and subtraction,
having to face a whole hurricane
without their parents.

Did you see the line of children leaving
the school, hands to shoulders
as they'd been told?
Did you think the terrible thought:
We should've taught them to scatter and squat
like marines in a battle
else he'd pick them off back to front
the way hunters cull a line of ducks

I don't want to be thinking this.
I don't want to crawl into bed either.
I want to raise my hand and ask
good questions, like

Are they together?
Is there a heaven?
Have the tulips bloomed there too?
Do they find pretty stones there and little feathers
that they return calling O cherub, Mrs. cherub
you dropped your feather because
do they love the bubbles in that word

                                    cherub?

The word clip, in contrast, has
quick metal and theft in it but it's not right
late night radio says: clips just
hold and feed (I don't wanna see this)
hold and feed
bullets into a magazine. Magazine
is the correct term. Saying clip in fact is proof
you don't know what you're talking about.

I don't know what I'm talking about.
So I better add and subtract
until I get the right answer, like

  13 days till Christmas
+ 2 more days of Hanukkah
= about 101 packages
someone had to deal with.

Minus 3 to 11 bullets per body—but
now we're on to multiplication
and they never made it on to
multiplication, did they? Like

   5 fingers
x 40 hands
x all the parents grandparents aunts and uncles
who once traced each tiny finger
as if it were an indivisible, indelible-ink miracle
= oh...about a Bazillion!

Now times that by 4—
for the four teachers who went
with them
divided by 3—the 3 guns that came
with him
multiplied by 2—the principal, the school psychologist
divided by 1
mother
teaching a son
to take aim and fire,
never thinking hurricane
never dividing number of bullets in a magazine
by the number in a line of cherubim leaving
us

with the zero of a gun muzzle,
heart silencer on

and zero times any number
(as they would have learned
later) always equals—we need to see this—zero

Sketch for a Hummingbird

I wanted to write about that hummingbird
lighter than a dime. I thought I had to wade
through a little mud first, a rutted somehow.
On the Long March, the cold
deep marshes of Sichuan Province
swallowed hundreds. If you sank
to your chest, an old comrade
remembered, they left you, they knew:
inextricable. Self pity
is a cold deep, bitterness too
of course. I wanted to say a few things
about extrication—lives popping
like corks from champagne, auditions
gone viral, miners rising in the miraculous capsule,

and alcoholics in their closing circles like a beneficent uranium
releasing, round the clock, serenity, serenity
and wisdom. The pictograph
of the old man's face read
friends, friends, hands.
Did he go back, risk the breath
of last words to take a tiny,
three–chambered heart between his teeth—
a city, a street, an unborn baby's name?
Lot's wife only looked back.
The farmers who found it must have heard
or dreamed they did
the terra–cotta army of Emperor Qin
humming, humming its way to excavation.

If gay marriage had been legal for me I'd be divorced twice, at least, and I'd have a house

Celia, you know I would have gone down on one knee
and given the four chambers of my heart to you
in a setting made of the circle of all my years
and you would have said no and I would have known
sooner. I should have let you give me
the VW, should have given you
the cat. You know my family never asked
What happened to that Celia?
Five years. Did your father ask about that shiksa
who blushed so easily? I still have
the little Yiddish he gave me, still have him.

Diane, I know you loved me. In Colorado,
when we lay on that house of a boulder watching a summer storm
cross the plain like a ship of lightning
you might have asked what could not then in any state
be asked and I would have said maybe
and we might have changed
sooner. Thank you for teaching my brother
to use your camera. Thank you for sending the pictures
when he died. Thank you for the picture of him
you keep in your mind.

Kaki. Six tiny diamonds from my great aunt Helen's ring,
three to each silver band to unite us in the holy
river of our state
park campground, where the current
knocked us nearly over. A job
the years completed. I call you X,
call you often, call you friend.
Not long ago I had a great blue heron
inked into my back, for a big birthday
I thought, but the blades of grass,
meant to show the heron hunting in a marsh, came out
an X over and through that heron's heart,

divorce papers from a universe that knows
we were married. I don't do commitment
very well I guess but maybe if I'd had
the decorated hall, the layered cake, the guts
to ask or be asked, to say no, yes, wait, change…
Oh what does it matter? Marriage equality
comes too late for me. It's a summer storm I watch
alone on a boulder, counting
not the seconds between lightning and thunder's climax
but the alternate universes that keep remorse
so busy.

To the Guy Holding the *Jesus Hates Fags* Sign

Who shot you up with the Novocain of hatred
and extracted your brotherly love?
Hate and Jesus in the same sentence?
Makes about as much sense
as the Mars Rover on Venus
as the Venus de Milo in Las Vegas neon
as Neo taking the blue pill

But you must be brave
standing there in your polyester slacks
clutching that sign like a hatchet
in a zombie attack
like a rope out the shark tank
like your life's last hard on
on a street streaming
with slam poets
who'd like to slam dunk you
into a port-a-john

at a prune festival.
Maybe brave enough to hear
what I have to say
so I say it: Every day of his life,
every night of his lie
my father stuck his head
through the noose of a bottle,

which is a very small noose
almost weddingband sized
but it worked—not as fast
but just as final
as Tyler Clemente's
bridge too high.

What a shame that being ashamed
of being gay trans bi
never goes out of style. My father
was handsome, a leader, a quarterback, a dancer
and damn you, Jesus loves him
prolly hauled buns across the halls of heaven
just to welcome him
with a kiss, to tell him
what I'm about to tell you
you bigoted son of a bitch:
Your sign is a lie.
I hope and pray you don't cement someone today
into a closet of self hate
that becomes a casket.
And yes I have been saved, thank you.
God led me to my lover and told me
love her openly and well
and neither of them ever had a problem
with the other.

It's you who's got the problem chump.
Heterosexual marriage is in trouble
cause we're not all heterosexual
and fake it till you make it
don't make it with the heart
unless the heart's gone numb

You look a little numb yourself son.
Prolly not brave enough to answer
what I have to ask yet I ask it:
Were you ever afraid
were you ever afraid you're gay?
Did they call you faggot?
And is that why you clutch that sign
like a snake that would bite you
like a clue that would screw you
like a rope
that would hang you
if you let it.

I am Troy Davis

At 11:08 PM 9/21 2011
the state of Georgia
took my life by lethal injection
and I was innocent.

But don't believe me.
Believe the death row guard
who pleaded with my sister
Don't cry so hard Martina.
We trying to keep it together ourselves.

Yeah the mothers of the guards
were praying for a stay,
people round the world sayin'
If this not reasonable doubt
doubt lost its reason

You know Billy Holiday wrote
after every time she sang "Strange Fruit"
she had to throw up.
Georgia when you gonna stop this?
Georgia Ray Charles even ashamed.
Georgia how do you sleep at night?
How does it feel to be Pontius Pilate?

Wait, I'm not sayin I'm like Christ.
I was just a guy in the wrong place
at the wrong time
with the right complexion face.
I was just a man
they laid on the cross three times
and three times held the hammer aloft,
nail all lined up
then gonna say oh not...yet.
And death row's not torture?

Naw, I'm not like my Lord but lord
my death ought to end death as a penalty,
because the state makes mistakes
and some states parole boards stocked with cops
not inclined to clemency,
because each life holds a light
the darkness brings to life
as night does the stars,
because racism's as American
as the wall captured Africans built
to keep Native Americans
off the Europeans
trying to steal Manhattan.
Yeah I'm talking about Wallstreet. I do read.

Did you read how, with my lastmost sentence,
I'll ask God to have mercy on those who killed me?
Because it's not about vengeance,
it's about justice, and behind justice, love.

Like those guards who became my friends—
they've already got issues, they're not getting over this.
And the family of the officer that was shot…
no peace, no peace for them when they realize
they were fiendin' after an innocent Christian
and the guilty man's been free
twenty-three years.

Course I worry most about my little nieces, my nephs,
like Antone, Antone Davis Correia—
he won this big award at the Georgia Social Studies Fair
for *How does the death penalty affect our state?*
I was so proud.
Is he having nightmares now
about my last fifteen minutes?

Oh they inject something
paralyzes your muscles
but only us who left death row death-first know
does it paralyze the rest,
the nerves and the brain,

all the parts that feel pain.
Does a minute last
an hour, do the senses turn
superpower?

And I did hear something
coming from a distance...
like a choir when you're you-know
running late, still like half a block
from the church...*We are*,
I thought I heard, *Troy Davis*.
Yes, that's what it was: We are Troy Davis.
Amazing. I never thought I'd be famous.
They put my voice on lockdown but lookout now
it's crossed oceans, getting work done in languages
I don't even know.

I guess if sharing my name with a lot a good people
helps end this death penalty mess then go on
chant your hearts out
or should I say
chant them in:

We are Troy Davis
(come on)

We are Troy Davis
(that's it)

We are Troy Davis
(I got this)

Rodrigo

"On October 12th, a sailor called Rodrigo saw the early morning moon shining on white sands, and cried out...The first man to sight land was supposed to get a yearly pension of 10,000 Maravedis for life, but Rodrigo never got it. Columbus claimed he had seen a light the evening before. He got the reward."

—from Howard Zinn's *A People's History of the United States*

What ten thousand Maravedis even once
might have meant to me
but I have lived

have lain among my bunkmates
swaying like a mango on a richly laden tree

have prayed for water and been given water.
I know more than he
about men and the length of the sea.

Some nights it was possible to walk
back unbent, a mother's son among the stars.

Abiding stars!
Whose spaces pried my ribs apart
I call on you—

did I not see moonlight lay its face
upon that breast of sand?

Women
less frequent than hurricanes.
Boll weevil bread, labor under the lash.

No wonder death comes so soon so

toothless in Madrid.

The beggar drags his dead leg down the alley.

My window is rich with rooftop and sky.

I did not cry out at once
but paused one moment
to count what I would have

for that moment only: a wife , a house, a grove
a son whose hand I'd guide along a row
daughters bringing figs

figs and wine.
Is it the beggar's leg scrapes so
or my breath?

Thirty-three days at sea.
Dawn saw them
swimming out to greet us

from sand white as an altar cloth
before the blood of his dis–
covery soaked it through.

Have mercy on me Oh Lord but do to him
as you will.

The beggar stops beneath my window.
Rodrigo, Rodrigo

The stars know, the stars know.

The Gentlemen of the Doctrine
a blackout poem

With words and word order from The Requerimiento, a 16th Century document written by the Spanish crown and read by Conquistadors, in Spanish, to Native Americans.

1

On behalf of barbarous peoples
we their servants make known
our Pope, who
as Lord of the Earth
gave these islands and mainlands
and the Ocean Sea
to every described desire.

Force will make war
in every place and by every means.
We will take you, your wives and children
and make them slaves.

We will do evil and avow death

2

Receive your own blame
Gentlemen. Come with us.

As Free as that Free

Columbus was a rapist and a pedophile
I call on white people everywhere
to say it

Oh Freedom you still feel like an American invention
to me, all my uncles short, soft-hearted men
who feared their mothers and ruined their backs
by 40, fought in the wars, swallowed their stories,
cast their hearts on the wind

The wind I give my face to is an American wind.
I want to be patriotic and honest
at the same time

But Columbus was a rapist and a pedophile
and all our wealth is built on blood.
When I call on white people everywhere to say it
they hate me

It is better to be hated than to pretend

Oh freedom you still feel like an American invention
to me—Whitney's big, good-job-guys! wave to the stadium,
her honest smile and that octave-leap note—sweet Jesus
we'll remember it in our DNA

and I don't think
she even gave us all she had

I think she gave us
just a taste

Oh freedom forgive us
Oh Friends
friends and lovers forgive us
Oh enemies forgive us

Maybe we can never be friends
Maybe you can never love us
despite the drum major's
gospel eloquence
but don't become us
don't become us
I can tell you in advance
it's not nice

Our children despise us
Our grandchildren love true style
and truth too much

Columbus was a rapist and a pedophile
I call on white people everywhere to say it

I call on Ukrainian Italian
German Belgian French Finnish Irish
Polish Czech Latvian Spaniard Portuguese
all you pale people
Sweden and Denmark too
and you, England, you killer
all you Conquistadors
and settlers
smallpox carriers

Quit with the priest jokes
and say it: Christopher Columbus
was a rapist and a pedophile
He gave girls and boys to his guys
He did not cherish their inner light
and all our wealth
all our wealth
is built on slavery

When you can state that
fact white America
when you can start down the long hallway of other facts

each one a door opening onto a long hallway of doors opening onto hallways

of a mansion whose ground floor
we been living in in luxury
not noticing
the screams
not noticing
the blood
running down the walls
like a mighty stream

When you've explored
the whole haunted house of our history
white America then maybe
you can sing a note as true
as Whitney sang
as free as that

                    free

Magical Thinking

That the mail brought nothing this morning because last night
I saw the full moon through a screen door and didn't
open the screen door

That lilacs whoosh their fragrance toward us on purpose and the breeze
abets this

That the orange koi rising from the murk of the pond pauses at the ladder's fourth rung
for a reason

That forgetting the names of wildflowers is dangerous

That a heron flying low directly overhead answers any pressing question
with Yes, of course yes!

That the date on a penny I find marks the year my life turned 'round

That a supernova explosion accelerates the openings of mystics
and was accelerated by them

That the black snake trapped and strangling in plastic lattice
called forth the dream—a black snake free

Or would you have it that the things and moments of this world
mean nothing, are as a semi's eighteen wheels singing and singing
to none but the deer dead on the shoulder and the living ones
timing their leaps

Looking Up

Things were looking down
last November. I had writer's block. Who could blame me—
all these young poets coming up
with more skills than Whitney had Grammys?
Plus it was getting dark at, what, like four o'clock?
I had to go for a walk
just to puts some distance between my mouth
and my chocolates.

And on that walk jeese louise
these geese were honking like a son-of-a-gun!
I had to look up—a big Nike swoosh, right there!
I could see each goose,
then, in matter of minutes,
diminished to an eyelash
over the Catskills.

I was amazed. I had to go google
How does that gaggle travel so damn rapid? Oh yeah
tag team strategy—each bird takes a turn
pumps to the front
bears the brunt of the wind
to the max of its capacity
then drops back as another moves up.
And that honking we hear—
it's actually encouragement,

Work those wings girl, keep it up son,
that's it, thank you, think south south so-outh . . .
and they don't get a lot a resistance
from emo nonsense
like anger and resentments
over wetlands mauled by malls
meadows all condo sprawl
ponds once common as quarters in a wishing well
now gone, gone *Oh hon, there's one . . .* gone,
don't indulge nostalgia
for the caterpillar cornucopia
that used to open, cocoons hatching
just as the famished flock touched down,
a miracle of timing,
the planet like an Italian grandmother
busy in the kitchen
before you even choose her address on the GPS
like a Puerto Rican tia busy making pastelillos
before you're even up and dressed
like a Jewish grandmother
going crazy with the keugle
before you even said *yes, we're coming*
as if God knows geese,
each goose by name,
strung their needs like beads on a string
and wears it all the time.

Hey, admit you're amazed,
how they find their way back
the same mates to the same slim dock
how if one drops out, injured, sick or shot
two more escort it to the ground and wait
no matter what—could be the middle of the city
could be a hunting club—wait
for recovery
or death.

Oh death, wait . . . do you look up
when you hear the geese?
Do you raise your gaze from problems and pain
to see victory, peace and victory in those V's,
to receive the promises I have received
and which nature always makes—
that what leaves comes back
that when we leave we don't have to leave alone
that unseen roads lead home and cycles
rock us like cradles, cycles
rock us like cradles

because God knows *us*
by name, been studying our needs
since the first nanosecond of that
Big dang ain't we *still* looking up
and back amazed at it

                                    Bang

What Grace is For

This is for my brother Joey
who played amazing grace on a plastic recorder so long one day
I told him *Enough, enough with the Amazing Grace!*

He was practicing fingerings to play it on the bagpipes
at our sister's wedding.
He was 16 and a half.
I never saw him a...

...a green t-shirt that read *A Boy of Quality is not Afraid of a Girl for Equality*
Yeah I gave it to him but he wore it all the time that time we camped out west
and he posed on the grand damn canyon edge flailing and faking a fall.
Made my stomach fall
on a hand grenade
as if I knew
as if I could save any...

one mother by her fifth gets a little worn out

so I got up with him some nights, rocked him, rocked him till he drifted off—
tomgirl toughgirl but girl
me and my baby brother bonded
better than Lady Gaga
    and high heels
better than Michelle Obama
    and deltoids
better than Barry Bonds
    and steroids
better than Lance Armstrong
    and lies

One time we found these baby rabbits
all minkly soft in a bowl of meadow.
He pleaded could we take one home,
I told him Joey, they're too young
and think of the mother   when she finds one gone

When our mother found him gone
grief tore her gut Alien–like
and predator cancer hauled the U–Haul on in.
She didn't last long

He died in the cabin of a dry-docked boat
with smoke   and flames
and his best friend

and you can bet I heard that song 500 times
and heard that song 500 more
just to be the one on the floor
in the puddle of guilt and regret forever–
(I'm talking a Edgar Allen Poe level of ever here) more

where I found out
I found out
what grace is for

So this
is for Amazing Grace
which my brother Joey played all day that day
working it even while waiting on line for a Big Mac and fries
like he was trying to bless the grease
trying to thread those irritating beeps
into beads
trying to finish
        an unfinishable piece

I was his hero.
If he was here Oh I think he'd say
Get up off that floor
and make something outcha grief
now that you know what grace is
what grace is

that saved a–a…

        is for

Notes

Part 1

"This Yes," page 6. Along with "Know Thyself," "Drops the
Spine," "Practice Cohoes Lacks," "The Great Peacemaker,"
"The Sea Knew a Small Sigh" and "One Light for Lucille,"
this poem is a cohonna, a form created for this book. A
cohonna consists of five or seven four-line stanzas of
diminishing lines; each stanza ends in a single word or
phrase. A last stanza (the sixth or eighth) is a one-line
envoi gathered from all the stanzas' last word(s), in order,
punctuation open.

"America the Beautiful, America the Tomb" page 14.
Herman Wallace died on October 4th at the age of 71
three days after being released under court order from
Louisiana's Angola Prison, where he had been held in
solitary confinement for 41 years. The judge who released
him declared him innocent of the charge of killing a
prison guard. Wallace had helped organize a Black Pan-
ther chapter and worked to desegregate the notorious
prison.

"The Clotheslines of Cohoes" page 24. "America" appears
in *Howl and Other Poems*, by Allen Ginsberg.

"#lineswritten@cohoesfalls" page 30. After *Lines Written*

at the Cohos [sic], or *Falls of the Mohawk River* by Thomas Moore (1779–1852). Moore was an Irish poet, musician and activist, sometimes called Ireland's national bard. After his travels in the U.S. at the start of the 19th century he wrote essays condemning slavery. He once challenged a critic of such an essay to a duel. The opening of *Lines Written at Cohos*:

> From rise of morn till set of sun
> I've seen the mighty Mohawk run;
> And as I markt the woods of pine
> Along his mirror darkly shine,
> Like tall and gloomy forms that pass
> Before the wizard's midnight glass

From *The Complete Poems of Sir Thomas Moore*.

"The Great Peacemaker" page 32. "And at the top of the tree sits Skajina, the eagle. He watches all ways and will warn us when he sees approaching that which brings destruction and death." "The Peacemaker." Iroquois Indian Museum, n.d. Web. 22 Aug. 2013. <http://www.iroquois-museum.org/PEACEMAKER.htm>.

"The Spinner's Retort" page 40. "Souper" is a derisive term originating in The Great Hunger of 1845–52 (known outside

Ireland as The Potato Famine) for those who accepted soup from Protestant groups at the cost of conversion.

"The Sea Knew a Small Sigh" page 44. The lines "The name comes they say / from a Mohawk family falling / over the edge" refers to a European misunderstanding of the word Cohoes (Ga–ha–hoose), perhaps first recorded in *The History of Cohoes, New York, from its earliest settlement to the present time* (1877) by Arthur H. Masten.

Part 2

"Are You Really Working Class?" page 62. The phrase "that is fucking awesome" is sung, with *this not that*, by TeeWanz (Michael Wansley) on the song "Thrift Shop" by Macklemore and Lewis.

"Rodrigo" page 92. Sailors on Columbus's first voyage earned from 2000–4000 Maravedis a year, so a pension of 10,000 m per year would have been quite luxurious.

"Gentlemen of the Doctrine" page 96 is made of words taken in order from The *Requerimiento*. The *Requerimiento* was written by lawyers for the Spanish crown ca. 1511 and read to Native Americans (in Spanish) by Conquistadors such as Hernando de Soto in Florida.

Passages from The *Requerimiento*, with "blacked out" text crossed out.

"On behalf of the ~~king and the queen, subjugators of~~ barbarous peoples, we, their servants~~, notify and~~ make known ~~to you as best we are able, that God,~~ Our ~~Lord, living and eternal, created the heavens and the earth, and a man and a woman, of whom you and we and all other people of the world were, and are, descendants. Because of the great numbers of people who have come from the union of these two in the five thousand years which have run their course since the world was created, it became necessary that some should go in one direction and that others should go in another. Thus they became divided into many kingdoms and many provinces, since they could not all remain or sustain themselves in one place.~~

~~[....]~~

~~One of the past~~ Popes ~~who succeeded Saint Peter,~~ as Lord of the Earth gave these islands and mainlands of the Ocean Sea ~~[the Atlantic Ocean]~~ to ~~the said King and Queen and to their successors, with~~ every~~thing that there is in them, as is set forth in certain documents which were drawn up regarding this donation in the manner~~ described~~, which you may see if you so~~ desire.

[....]

~~If you do not do this, however, or resort maliciously to~~ ~~delay, we warn you that, with the aid of God, we will~~ ~~enter your land against you with~~ force ~~and~~ will make war in every place and by every means ~~we can and are able,~~ and we will ~~then subject you to the yoke and authority of the Church and Their Highnesses. We will~~ take you ~~and~~ your wives and children and make them slaves~~, and as such~~ we ~~will sell them, and will dispose of you and them as Their Highnesses order. And we will take your property and~~ will do ~~to you all the harm and~~ evil ~~we can, as is done to vassals who will not obey their lord or who do not wish to accept him, or who resist~~ and ~~defy him. We~~ avow ~~that the~~ deaths ~~and harm which~~ you will receive ~~thereby will be~~ your own blame~~, and not that of Their Highnesses, nor ours, nor of the~~ gentlemen ~~who~~ come with us."

From Jerald T. Milanich and Charles Hudson, *Hernando de Soto and the Indians of Florida* (Gainesville: University Press of Florida, 1993), 36–37.

116

Colophon

This book and cover were designed by
Baohouse LLC. The content is typeset in
ITC Officina Sans.